Scent of betrayal

Love in the Civil War

Violeta Karampini

Amazon Kindle Direct Publishing

Contents

Dedicated to those who have truly fallen in love,

Preface

Love, friendship, hatred, ideologies and mixed feelings in Toledo, Spain a few years before the start of the Spanish Civil War. Two friends Alejo and Felipe grow up in an environment of turmoil, inseparable from their childhood and yet the events reveal their real characters. How will the beautiful Catalina live her choices? Who will win in the end friendship, love, or betrayal? What choices will the heroes make in a country like Spain of socio-political change? The purpose of this book is to highlight emotions, characters and not to narrate historical events. Two friends, a woman and different ideological backgrounds in a story with heroes who are the product of fiction and are placed in the real historical context of the Spanish Civil War. How can the horror of a war irreparably hurt the lives of our heroes?

The Letter

April 1935, Toledo

Dear Catalina,

I feel happy just to know that you are reading this letter. I feel lucky just to have you holding in your warm hands full of love and affection a letter of mine. There are so many things I want to express to you that this piece of paper and pencil help me even slightly to capture them in time. No morning dawns that I do not wake and no dusk that I do not rest without your memory. The days, the hours, the minutes pass slowly and torturously until I meet you again and see your pure smile. There is no power that can separate me from you, my dear. I don't know what fate has in store for us, all I know is that you are the reason I live and breathe. It saddens me to think that one day your love for me may dry up but even then I will still continue to loving you.

Yours,
Alejo

I have always been possessed by a curiosity to discover new things but this time my curiosity led me to something quite old. How exciting to find a piece of paper yellowed and yet has stood the test of time and hides a piece of information within it. But in my case, it kept an old story.

Grandma had never been angry or scolded me when I touched her things, so I figured she wouldn't mind if I read a personal letter of hers now either. It was hidden so deep in the bedroom dresser that someone would think it had been dropped there and forgotten. Grandma Catalina was a cheerful and hospitable person, with a heart of gold and a sweet soul. I still carry with me the memories I have of her. She would talk to me, sing to me and I still remember the fruit we would pick to make jam. On our walks she would show me different flowers and explain every single question i had as a child. Of course, there was no shortage of our little secret of giving me sweets and treats. I loved looking at pictures <<from the old days>>. So, every time I opened grandma's album of black and white photos, I loved to gaze at moments of memories she had with grandpa. They were an elegant couple of another era classier with charm and respect. Grandpa was exuberant and condescending but grandma always had a brooding look that she tried to hide behind her bright smile. I touched these photos, smelled them and felt each time that I was holding a lifetime in my hands. But was I only seeing a moment and not the whole life? Was I seeing it this way as a granddaughter? The truth is that this letter further strengthened this suspicion, but perhaps it only influenced me to doubt.

So I sat by the bed with silk sheets sewn in Bruges, Belgium with such a delicate texture and soft feel as the unparalleled character of this city and began reading with the curiosity of my youth. Holding an old letter brought me in touch with the written way of communication of people of another era. I immediately sensed that it was a love letter to my grandmother, Catalina. This recording of emotions, this hope, love and tender moments made me feel a sense of peace but also somewhat red with shame to read something so personal of my grandmother and then something strange and uncomfortable happened. Who is this Yours truly? Who is this man who wrote so romantically?

In my hands I was holding a love letter full of emotion and nostalgia for the old days when the manuscript had its own glamour and a story of love, pain or anticipation to narrate you. As I was immersed in thinking about who the mysterious romantic man was, I heard footsteps approaching me. The floor of the house was made of wood and time had worn away its quality so that when someone walked there was a slight creaking sound as if it were summer cicadas talking incessantly to our summer memories. I glanced toward the sliding door and discerned the figure of my mother approaching me. That day we had both come together as usual to tend to grandma's garden that she loved so much. It was the most blooming and musky garden of all in Toledo. Full of rose bushes in different colors white, pink, red. Each time the garden offered you the same feeling of being in a natural environment so vibrant and so alive. I always remember on celebrations grandma Catalina would decorate the house with roses in vases and prepare traditional local sweets. That taste of it took you on a sensory path. The hall with its crystal objects and floral wallpaper was filled with people and grandmother and grandfather as hosts welcomed friends and relatives in a festive atmosphere and somehow seemed classy to my childhood eyes at the time.

Mother sat next to me with her wonderfully expressive eyes that she had inherited from grandma. She glanced at the love confession I gave her and had that look of surprise as you try to interpret what was going on. Then on her face I saw a smile of the kind that betrays the existence of some perhaps forgotten memory. It was that smile printed on the mother's lips that bore witness to the story that had been forgotten for years. Mother had the magical ability of a wordsmith because whenever she struggled to tell me a story from the past, her descriptions were so eloquent that you would think you were the protagonist of the story. A story where life in that era is like the ones we read in novels.

-The truth is that this letter is a piece of grandma Catalina's heart. I am impressed that it has remained in the cupboard for so many years without being destroyed. The material may have worn away but I believe its contents will remain forever.

-But who is Alejo, mother?

I was surprised with a look of an investigator wanting to decipher her words but I was eager to know who this man in love was. I have always loved stories of strong love and the mere idea that there may have been something similar in our family increased my thirst to hear something romantic with intensity.

-Life is full of good and bad moments like love is not just the words you read but moments that are indelible over time. In all of these moments, however, we may be called upon to confront choices.

The first years

I n Toledo, in the community of La Mancha - Castile, where life was like a fairy tale of the golden age, the inhabitants lived in harmony. The city of three cultures, as it was called because of the coexistence of Christians, Jews and Muslims, was destined to suffer great destruction during the Spanish Civil War. The medieval aspect of the province of Toledo gives the sense of a journey through time where the past creates a unique experience and combines the chivalric element with the embrace of the Tagus River. It is well known that in the region artists, amazing creators, made swords and various artifacts that were the jewels of the culture and praise for their manual skills.

Toledo has always been an inspiration for a painting. Alejo always recognized this magical element and never missed the opportunity to capture the beauty of nature, even with a simple pencil or paints sent to him by aunt Maria Carmen from Paris. Aunt Maria Carmen was married to a French merchant of the time and after their marriage, as the mores of the time dictated, she followed him home. Their age difference never prevented aunt Maria Carmen from being devoted to her husband. He adored her and proved it to her every time she asked to visit Spain to meet her family and bring them all those gifts that in cosmopolitan Paris were an everyday occurrence. But aunt Maria Carmen's travels were becoming fewer and fewer because of the spanish flu pandemic and the ongoing political unrest in Spain. As a teenager Alejo spent time during the summer months on his family's farm in Toledo. He loved reading and painting with his fascination with nature already being a source of inspiration in the various landscapes he depicted with the paints at his disposal.

The farm was one of the finest in the county, full of all kinds of varied flowers. It looked like a dream and the smells of the flowers made the atmosphere unforgettable. The lush green grass covered the entire garden where flowers and various fruits and vegetables pranced around adorned with their blossoms and buds. Their intoxicating fragrance was an attraction for the colorful butterflies as well as the worker bees, who lost no time in flying from flower to flower. Alejo's father had planted a wide variety of fruit and vegetables in order to have enough for the family's consumption.

Alejo's father, Don Lorenzo Carranza practiced the profession of a teacher and taught in a school in his province Toledo. He loved knowledge and learning very much and never took the opportunity to bombard his only son with information as well as examining him. He was an only child and his parents were very fond of him and always saw to it that in addition to becoming a proper man of respect he became a proper man of his own free will. His mother, Doña Sophia Olmenda Carranza, was an excellent mother and wife. She was the best seamstress in all of Toledo. With her needle and thimble she had done wonders. There was not woman in the area who was not elegant and well-dressed because of her talent of Doña Sophia, she even sewed high quality fabrics brought to her by aunt Maria Carmen from the City of Light. Alejo was sure that he had inherited from his mother her big black eyes and also her patience.

In the outskirts of the walled city of Toledo was the church of San Tome, where on Sundays and on holidays were celebrated services for the faithful. It is known that this church is adorned with the famous work of Dominikos Theotokopoulos, the oil painting of the famous El Greco <<The Burial of the Count of Orgaz>>. All the families of the area attended the Mass and after the end of the Mass the inhabitants would gather in Plaza de Zocodover, which is the main square and the center of the town. Alejo was meeting with his best friend Felipe Meneses. They had known each other since childhood, although being a friend not only means knowing each other for many years but they had a true friendship something rare and priceless like a precious gift. Always honest with each other, they supported each other, they may have come from different family backgrounds, but their friendship was like aged wine that does not fade easily. And if sometimes there were tensions everything was overcome on the basis of reason and communication, or was it not all?

Felipe Meneses was also a charming young man like his friend with several qualities in his personality and a gentle demeanor, he was like a gentleman of the time. Intelligent, active and sure of himself, he may not have had the same interest in farm work and the gifts of nature as Alejo but he would always help his friend with a difficult farm task. He was a boy full of ambition and dreams. His family was one of the best known and most commendable in the country. His father Don Pedro Meneses did particularly important social work as he was a general doctor. In every emergency he was present in order to save human life. Felipe was quite similar to him in appearance as he was as tall with brown hair and just barely beginning to make an appearance of a distinctive moustache that testified to his age. The one characteristic that set him apart was that Don Pedro was a despotic man and quite persistent when it came to imposing his point of view. In contrast, his mother, Doña Orora, had her roots by a rich family of the time with aristocratic habits. Her father was a banker, and from the love he had for his youngest daughter he combined his job with Orora's name (oro - gold). Doña Orora was a woman of harmonious characteristics, with inner peace and tranquility. She was one of the best-dressed ladies of the province. Alejo's mother sewed her dresses that showed splendor and were always combined with glove hats and jewelries as the style of the time dictated. A style consisting of luxurious clothes and fabrics that evoked admiration for the enhancement of femininity and beauty.

It was logical for the time that such a family was considered to belong to the upper classes after all, and their residence was in keeping with their social profile. It consisted of two floors and was built of stone and wood, the lower floor was intended to receive visitors and consisted of an inner patio and many rooms. One of these chambers was arranged in such a way as to serve the needs of a dispensary where Don Pedro received their patients. However, life in the house flourished in the inner atrium where visits were made by high-ranking people from the region and the country itself. The doctor received friends, politicians and government officials, diplomats and military officers. They would spend hours discussing matters concerning the political turmoil facing the country and the dangers of a hazardous schism. Don Pedro was particularly absolute and liked to be in control of situations not only within his family but also for his own country.

Besides, the political scene of those years was particularly fragile due to a series of fragmented governments that frustrated the king, combined with the failure of the army in Morocco.

-*Father, I see you looking anxious and thoughtful lately. What is troubling you?*

Felipe asked Don Pedro one day as he felt his anxiety but knew he was always well informed.

- *At the moment there is no concern son, but Felipe we must be prepared for everything. The situation may get out of hand we must be ready to protect your mother and your little sister, Magdalena. I have a feeling that unprecedented events await us.*

He replied in a somewhat troubled and doubtful tone.

Felipe and his friend Alejo were not discussing matters that he overheard in his father's conversations with high-ranking officials, or at least they were not yet on their minds.

At first glance

The 1931 Constitution had inaugurated the first true Democracy in the Iberian Peninsula country. The king's departure from power changed the balance of power and new reforms including the separation of church and state exuded an air of revitalisation. Manuel Azaña of the Republican and Socialist party advocated modernizing the country to distance itself from the monarchical powers and pursue a path to development. The newspapers of the time in their news coverage documented all thess changes but there was also a dissatisfied side that included corps of Officers - Spanish society was in turmoil.

- Every time I read this yellow mag I am overcome by the same reflection. This progressive government has created enemies not only in the monarchical and ecclesiastical bodies, but also has enemies within its own party under the pretext that it has not fulfilled everything it has promised to do.

exclaimed Alejo who always had the seed of curiosity in him and was informed about the volatile social situation in Spain.

- My good friend Alejo, the reforms that have been put in place require responsibility and proper handling. Surely whoever is in power will see to the welfare of our nation.

Felipe replied calmly and with a spirit of condescension without wanting to express his support for either side.

- How can you be so indifferent to power and the insolent threat to Democracy? Have you read what is happening with the extreme factions in Europe?

- I have been informed but what would satisfy me is unity, order and security in our society and not to support the division that threatens us. And because the mood has become too heavy I suggest we get up and walk in the alleys, it is a sunny day my friend to spoil our hearts.

Somewhat similar were their conversations when it came to the political turmoil in the country. They may have never resolved the issue of governance but both Alejo and Felipe did not argue vigorously in their disagreements. After all, they had had many experiences together as children, as they had now both temporarily settled in Madrid for their studies.

The Complutense University was one of the oldest institutions in the world. This large campus occupied a large part of Madrid. Naturally, Alejo had devoted himself to the educational process and in particular his love of history led him to pursue literature, on the other hand, Felipe, watching his father in the doctor's office, also discovered his own inclination towards medical science, he and his father may have had different views on political matters but in matters of a medical nature he was always present to talk and observe his techniques.

The lively capital of Madrid offered authentic moments of local daily life in the main square of the city and in the Plaza Mayor many events and markets took place. During their studies, Felipe and Alejo divided their free time between the public library, where they spent hours lost in the wealth of book knowledge, and the traditional shops and cafés that dominated the arcades of the capital. The arcades have always been places of social gathering and exchange of ideas for the inhabitants. A stroll among the tables lined up in the arcades would most often end up in a café where you could sip a hot drink and enjoy the intimate feel of a place filled with photographs on the walls of sailors' voyages.

In 1933, Christmas would have found the country of Spain

more divided and confused than ever before. A few months earlier, in September of that year, Azaña's progressive government fell. Democracy was collapsing and the danger of division was raging like a lion ready to devour its prey. In the mansion of the Meneses as well as in the farmhouse of Carranzas, a festive atmosphere prevailed. The joy was twofold not only because it was Christmas but because their lads had returned for the holidays. A festive atmosphere prevailed throughout the town with smells of food and dishes, in every neighbourhood in every family, but the celebrations were a parody as a two-year period of tears and discontent followed.

Already the first arbitrary acts had appeared, which suppressed the progressive steps of the previous years. Fascism was sweeping across Europe and the wave of hatred was not long in coming to Spain, where it was at a crossroads where the choice of a course was irreversible. The young people of the time, full of dreams and the optimism of their youth but also with the spontaneity of their youth, were forced to follow the developments of events and take a stand. But no one could have imagined that many would be carried away by the excessive ambition of the few. The emergence of extreme right-wing groups is further adding to the climate of insecurity and uncertainty.

On a regular walk where they spent hours discussing their concerns and dreams for the future, Alejo sank into the deep waters of happiness. He had never felt like this before, he felt a flame go through him. But how is it possible that one look could make him feel a feeling that burns your heart. But when he looked at her he understood that this love was not just a glance but in every glance. The look she gave him had so much value, so much brilliance that no sun would be as bright and shining as their persistent gazes. He knew that with this girl he would lose track of time. But how would he get close to her? It was a godsend when a small object fell from the girl's basket. Alejo immediately left Felipe standing in front of the bookstore where they were browsing through various books and ran towards the girl, who was accompanied by a plump lady who was very domineering.

-Pardon, you dropped something of yours.
He chanted in a trembling voice, looking at her in her big brown eyes.
- Thank you young man, that's very kind. Let's go, my daughter.
 He watched her walk downstairs and then he knew that this girl would mark him not only in his soul but in his very life.

She

H e wonder who the girl with the fiery eyes was? Was she a dream or reality? Did the dream look like reality or did reality look like a dream? The silence of her gaze hid the words the young girl did not say, but Alejo understood them. They returned home and his mind couldn't stop thinking about her. His soul was flooded with light and a storm of emotions stirred his being. He still brought to his mind her spicy smile and her enigmatic eyes. How else was it possible to forget such eyes full of vitality, passion and innocence. He had to find out in every possible way who this girl was, he wanted very much to see her again, to get close to her and lose himself in the enigma of her eyes.

In the earlier years everything went differently, even love had its unique special role. It was a gift that a select few would feel the true love that springs from the depths of the heart, burns your whole soul and stirs your body. Alejo felt that the mysterious vision would be the drop that would fill the entire sea of his heart. He was sure he wanted to see her again and get close to her, to talk to her. He felt from the first moment that with her he would experience the essence and not the surface. That night Alejo found it difficult to sleep, he was constantly thinking and lying awake.

Time froze in the second of her smile.

The black two-year period that had begun was a bastion of destruction. In 1933 all the steps of progress that had been established were being suppressed and in their place was a kind of aggressive policy aimed at tearing the subordinate working class to pieces. A great wave of reactions swept over the human indignation in its wake and in many Spanish cities demonstrations and workers' strikes broke out. In Asturias, the front of the struggle had broken out with vigour and determination. The uprisings were signalling bloody results and several families were forced to leave the capital Oviedo in order to avoid being fired upon by the raging bulls of indignation. Many were those who had to protect their families and especially their children from the government's wrath in the region. The same decision was followed by one of the judges in Oviedo, Ignacio Herrera, who asked to be transferred to the province of Toledo. He has not had many days since he has moved with his family to the city, he was a man of integrity, fairness and discipline with a love for the administration of justice. He and his wife Marta had created a close-knit family with respect and morality.

Don Ignacio Herrera wanted in every way possible to protect his family so that they would never again experience the horrible moments of a loss. A few years ago misfortune had met them on the doorstep of their lives, as the cursed disease of the time deprived them of their first-born son Manolo. Doña Marta's pain was unbearable but she took strength from her two remaining angels. Fernando filled the void of the family's lost son, alleviating even the slightest bitterness of a mother's bitterness, if such bitterness can be mitigated that is. But life and happiness in the home blossomed with the kindness of their young daughter, Catalina. Catalina meant pure as pure was the look in her eyes that nailed Alejo that morning in the marketplace.

Catalina was a beautiful girl with a beautiful soul full of love, respect and creativity, and her creativity was also evident to Alejo; one look was enough to express the world of her soul. Her face angelic with harmonious features. She was a graceful young lady of the time and the most seductive curve in her body was her smile. She was fascinated by music and was particularly fond of the piano. Through music she expressed herself, she felt it was an integral part of her life. However, in recent days, the melodies on the piano were different, one could say they were more emotional, they were like romantic melodies expressing love through the eyes of the soul. With her thin, long fingers she touched the piano keys and recalled that day that the cowards forget but the lovers want to repeat. It was impossible for her to forget the kind young man who with an explosion ignited love in her heart. Doña Marta who knew her daughter better than anything else in the world knew that now her eyes were smiling with love, joy and for the first time since the loss of her brother she saw happiness painted on the calm expression of her face. So mutual was all this attraction that though their bodies were apart, their minds and hearts were united.

Until the day he returned to Madrid for the rest of his studies, Alejo never missed a chance to wander the alleys of the market and search for the woman who would colour his life, but this effort was in vain. One day as he was returning home after the farm work he was doing with his father on the farm, something unexpected happened, the girl with brown curls, the girl he had then seen in the market, the girl he had been looking for so many days was at his house. Donya Sophia with her needle had just given to her only son an incredible gift. Doña Marta and Catalina that day had visited the Carranza household in order to sew some new silk dresses. Alejo was stunned looking at Catalina through the mirror where she was rehearsing her elegant blue dress, then she turned her gaze to Alejo and her stomach began to fill with the butterflies her mother told her about how she would feel when she met her great love.

- *Forgive me for entering so abruptly, I didn't know mother was expecting visitors.*

Alejo exclaimed, surprised and upset.

- *Son, may I introduce you to Doña Marta, wife of Judge Herrera and her daughter Catalina. They recently moved to our city from Oviedo.*

Alejo couldn't believe that in just a few minutes, he learned about the mysterious girl he had been looking for days.

- *Nice to meet you. Mother is a true master craftswoman will pamper you and satisfy you with her work.*

Sweet Catalina, confused as she was, was trying to hide the adrenaline rush she felt at this unexpected introduction.

- *'My Alejo, I will ask you, however, to retire to your chamber for a while until we finish rehearsing.*

His father had taught to be chivalrous with women so he gave a handshake to Doña Marta and her daughter and left, leaving Catalina herself entranced. Without being noticed by Doña Sophia and Doña Marta he winked at Catalina thus implying a promise that they would meet again and soon indeed.

The day before they left for Madrid, Alejo also confided his love to his friend Felipe. Felipe, being a good listener, heard every detail of the whole story and understood that his friend was so much in love and had the hope that every man in love radiates. Meanwhile, Felipe's little sister Magdalena has developed a friendship with Catalina which would help as a link for Alejo to secretly deliver a letter to her:

January 1934, Toledo

Miss Catalina,

Allow me to speak to you in the singular, I believe we can remove the fence of formality. They say that the angels in earth do not escape but it is certainly a great lie because I met my own angel here on earth and specifically in the glow of your eyes. Every time I look at you you cause a sweet chaos in me, but I am at the same time happy to receive the same spark from you. Unfortunately, I am forced to be away for a short time in Madrid, but this distance means nothing when you mean so much to the other person. I will write to you as much as possible and find a way to communicate, even if only secretly. I will wait until the next time I hear the sounds of the sky coming from your voice and get lost in the universe of your eyes. I hope you will wait for me too.

Enchanted,
Alejo

Love means...

S omehow an intimacy full of romance and anticipation developed between them. They constantly exchanged letters with each other and through simple words a love grew, a love born from a glance. As the months passed, the letters increased and the longing exceeded all expectations, Catalina stood for several hours by the window of her chamber, eagerly awaiting the appearance of the postman. Don Adrian was a tiny man with a kindly figure, every day on his bicycle and with a brown bag he rode through the neighborhoods of Toledo distributing various letters. The little young lady in love, upon seeing him, would immediately run to the front door to receive her secret from Don Adrian. Excitedly she would shut herself up in her chamber and read her love letter countless times thus feeling that she was holding a piece of her beloved Alejo with her, Catalina may have expressed herself through her compositions on the piano but when she answered her lover's letters she literally painted. She believed that with her music she would awaken his every sense but because this was impossible at that particular moment in time due to the miles that separated them she was convinced that she could stimulate his senses in another way. In one of his letters he had likened her to the blooming flowers in the garden of his house, so whenever Catalina sent him a letter she perfumed it with various flowers to bring back the memory of her.

Don Ignacio's family was deeply religious and reverently observed a humble way of life; they had great respect for the pastor of the Toledo church and invited him on Sundays for dinner and discussion of matters of faith that concerned him. They knew each other from Oviedo as Pastor Don Pascual grew up in those lands and it was only when he was ordained a clergyman that he left his hometown to serve the will of God in Toledo where many of different faiths coexisted, he considered it his duty to protect the faith of Christians. Catalina had great confidence in Don Pascual and in her confession she had mentioned Alejo as something pure that stimulated her faith in God's miracles on earth. Don Pascual felt the exultation that was in the young girl's soul and advised her never to lose hope of a life of happiness beside him.

In the summer of 1935 a year before the absolute horror in Spanish society, Manuel Azaña having been acquitted by the Court for the Protection of the Constitution began preparations to reform a new government so he helped to found the Popular Front of liberals, socialists and communists, all these preparations would become a reality in a few months. The news was spreading rapidly and the Spanish cities were becoming more and more divided, darkness was coming to cover with the few hopes of salvation that were fading faster and faster. Alejo during the preceding months had taken an active part in the developments and had formed his opinions, which were always in keeping with his revolutionary and impetuous character. Temporary tranquillity in the sea of indignation was given him by the thought of his only first love. After so long the moment came when he would see her again, the first time he could embrace her and breathe in her perfume. The date day had arrived and the desire had risen to the highest level that any lover has. Catalina wore her favorite blue dress the one that Doña Sophia had sewn for her that day of the first promise, her silky hair adorned with a white fabric ribbon that held back her wavy curls. She looked in the mirror and her heart was about to burst she had the excitement of a small child feeling the joy of a new toy.

Alejo was waiting for her near the bridge of San Martin in a spot away from the prying eyes of passers-by, he was very formal in matters of morality and in no way would he wish to expose a girl and insult her chastity before formally express his intentions to her family and Don Ignacio. The day was warm and from the sky the sun's rays pierced the atmosphere creating a mood that was in keeping with his romantic mood and suddenly as the sun peeked through the recesses of the bridge she appeared. In his eyes she lived the ideal, the absolute, he was so anxious: what he would say to her, how he would behave and he generally didn't know what to do so that sweet Catalina wouldn't be disappointed.

- *When you love someone, you wait, you endure and you persevere. All I need is your love to feel like a complete person.*
- *Your letters betray your soul and your love is the missing part of my life that I have always missed.*

He took her crystal fragile hands in his and cradled her in his arms. He may have held her in his arms for a short time but he knew he would hold her in his heart forever. He closed his eyes and just smelled her hair, always a man falls in love when he breathes in the scent of their beloved's hair wafting all those spring scents and the sounds of birds chirping framed the happiness they felt in each other's arms. Their eyes met and their bodies spoke, they were hungry for a kiss, their breathing grew heavy became sharp it was the perfect recipe for a first kiss but...

-*I propose to walk a little and enjoy the magic of the scenery.*

Alejo had done the right thing morally he didn't think it was appropriate to kiss the woman he loved on the first date, so he simply stroked her rosy cheek and they crossed the stone pathway between the lush green grasses. They talked about their lives, their families and even the political turmoil in the country. It was obvious that there was chemistry between them and a romantic tension that was increasingly uniting them in a love without denials. The end of this beautiful ride had come, Catalina had to return home immediately before her father noticed her absence when she returned from the market. Alejo accompanied her to a certain point kissed her hand and promised her that this would be the beginning of a beautiful adventure.

The next day, Alejo visited his friend Felipe at the doctor's office to tell him about yesterday's experience, he was after all his best friend and he only wanted to talk to him. Felipe, with his white robe that gave him prestige and the seriousness of science, was constantly mixing substances and preparing medicines and sedatives. He took off the hollow myopic glasses he wore so he could discern quantities and paused to listen to Alecho who came like a torrent into the laboratory ready to drown with his joy anything in his path.

- *I saw her, Felipe, I met her. She was so beautiful, so radiant that I thought I was in heaven. She's my whole world made me forget even the threat of being short-changed.*

- *That's good news. I'm glad, my friend, you finally found the woman who made you think about something beyond the race.*

- *Do you remember what my grandmother Doña Pakita used to say; when I find the love of my life everything will dissolve around me and I will see another reality. I feel it, Felipe, for this girl I'll fight anything, for her I'll give my life.*

- *I realized I have to work early in the morning because if you come here, you'll always have something to tell me. I suppose because I know you, you must have kissed her,, don't you?*

- *Of course not, I had her in my arms and I had everything. Her breath had a combination of cinnamon and caramel that lured me into her passion but you know how wrong it would have been once I met her. I wanted to get to know her more.*

Felipe had indeed guessed correctly Alejo after each date ran to his friend to confide in him about this unique experience he was having. Felipe was very happy that his friend, the brother he had never had was deeply in love and always in a good mood, he may have been a little jealous of this happiness in a good way as he felt that he too was missing a part of his life that would be filled by a woman full of love like the love Alejo was telling him about.

The narrative in which he became quite graphic was the moment he kissed the love of his life. It was a day like any other until the moment the young man in love would meet his adorable one and only Catalina. On their dates they used to talk, dream and observe but as he looked at her he felt like he was living his dream, but he was afraid of waking up and it was all in his imagination.

- My beloved, I want to be with you, to be a part of you, to serve your love.

- I don't just want to exist, I want to exist only for you.

it was so tender what she answered him so sincere to show her soul in a single phrase then Alejo turned to her he looked deep into her eyes, he shook himself dry and with a caress so loving he showed her that something magical was about to happen, something that would have worn him and her: a kiss. It was the most beautiful moment of his life his lips and her lips after so long were now joined, sealing their love, smiling and they both knew they were kissing the right person, it was the perfect kiss. That first kiss just proved the feeling that had been there all along, something special was being born between them. It was already getting dark, time to head back, but who can bear to be far from their destiny?

Life in a different way

As the months went by and the years rolled by, the two of them felt even happier and their love turned the bad days into meaningful days with a few drops of hope. The shadow of fear and strife had almost spread over the whole country, and hopes were scarce of appeasing the pro-war spirits. The two Spains were unfortunately already a fact in the geographical territory of the country. The situation had lately been out of control and political life within the borders had become dangerously polarised between the Left and the Right side; it was now certain that the history of Spain would record its darkest pages and no one would be left unscathed by the deadly ideological conflict. So many decades of entirely class-based conflict would culminate in a bloody Civil War. The number of casualties was already high enough before the war began and mass executions were continuing, Alejo felt more ready than ever to take a stand in the uprisings by openly pledging his support to the liberal bourgeoisie of the Republican forces of the left. The efforts of both Felipe and Catalina to prevent their involvement in the political conflicts were in vain:
- *We are at war you must understand I cannot stand impassive in the*

face of the unmitigated violation of my freedom.
- You don't understand Alejo they are at war and you just want to contribute to their excessive ambitions, you may not think of yourself, but your decision to fight puts your family at risk.

Felipe replied angrily at hearing Alejo's declaration to defend the forces of the left.

- You don't understand anything. You are locked in your sterile laboratory and you think that freedom is won with chemical compounds while outside the Nationalists are slaughtering innocent and civilian populations and without being in a state of war.
- For so many years the targets of attacks have been against the weak, you don't need to tempt fate and in addition from what you told me Catalina is not in agreement with your impulsive decision either.
 - Impulsive is in your eyes. So many young people are being trained to crush propaganda and fascism and even volunteers are arriving in the country to fight and to boost the morale of democratic fighters and you are cowing down to avoid problems.
- Cowardly about what exactly? Because you want to pretend to be a hero and you're going to get yourself killed putting your family in danger?
- I thought you were my best friend, but I can see how you disrespect my beliefs and the ideals I'm trying to uphold in the name of your subservient neutrality.

Alejo walked out of the doctor's office, slamming the heavy wooden door with force, causing a deafening sound that sealed a rift between a friendship of so many years. He wanted to fight, he was determined to help in the effort to crush and vanish once and for all the enemy. The thought of Catalina being free, safe and unafraid further convinced him of this decision.

On April 26, 1937, German and Italian interventions on the side of the Nationalists bombed the Basque town of Guernica, killing the civilian population. This attack strengthened the power of the Right wing, provoking the anger of the Left. The situation was now out of control. The noose was tightening around the populists of the left-wing Democratic government that was in power only a few months after its legitimate election. On July 17, 1936,

Spain was now bleeding, General Francisco Franco, who would lead the country into war and misery in the years to come, led his troops and mutinied against the government. The coup traumatized the government and the rebellion intensified. Spain was now divided in two. The Civil War had just begun. Alejo, along with other young men from Toledo and the surrounding provinces, had organized groups to fight for the Republicans. His relations with Felipe had cooled were now formal to nonexistent.

One night before he left for the field of hell he met his grieving lover in a secluded spot in the province to make his promises to her.

-*Honey, don't be unhappy, keep your tears to turn into tears of joy when we meet again. This war will end and I want us to be free. I have made you a promise and I will keep it, I leave my heart bound for you to hold. Without it a man cannot live, so I give it to you so that I may have an incentive to return to you and breathe.*

- *The quote from Charles Dickens that you quoted to me says that "the pain of parting is nothing compared to the joy of meeting again" I am proud of you and there on the city walls I hope you are thinking of me and writing to me.*

- *It is your thought that gives me the strength for the first time to do something for someone else and that someone else is you. I want you not to be afraid.*

This farewell was a moving farewell. Their kiss was wet with tears but the optimism that they would meet again was immense. Saying goodbye to each other was without a doubt one of the worst experiences two people in love could have, Alejo might be going away but inside him was Catalina. On the way back from their last meeting, from those encounters full of love, passion and romance, he embraced her and looked at her with a look of promise to return. The fact that they said goodbye should not mean the end of them, after all, anyone who loves takes care to keep his memory alive. Would the temporary distance confirm their deep feelings or would oblivion take its throne and eyes that are not seen are quickly forgotten?

In the early hours of the next morning, and in the utmost

secrecy, several Democratic supporters, and among them Alejo departed in a truck and armed with arms and supplies for the capital of the country, where the forces of the Popular Front were rallying together with the volunteers and the International Brigades to stimulate the democratic character of the city. Alejo, being educated and brave enough like the bull before the battle, was able to lead this group from Toledo and raise the morale of his countrymen who held on his backs to the Freedom of Spain. The siege of Madrid had just begun.

It was October 1936, when the defence of the city was supported by various forces loyal to the Spanish Republic. The battles in the various cities were breaking out one after another and the Nationalist army did not hesitate to open fire on women and children. Madrid held firm, the aerial bombardments instigated by Franco confirmed his identity as an enemy of the nation. But the anti-fascist reaction continued with the fighting being exhausting and constant slaughter on both sides. Alejo fought with his soul, giant with courage and bravery, the protagonist in his mind in every armed attack was his beloved for whom he fought. On the nights when they stopped hostilities with fatigue and suffering, the joy of the republicans was constantly raised when they succeeded in suppressing the attacks of the coup plotters, but how far would they be able to sustain the foundations of the Republic?

Soldiers, tanks, guns, planes reinforced all aspects of the Civil War. The worst selves, the baser instincts of the people, overlooked every good, every pure, every moral element in the life of the Spanish citizens. Few remained true to their ideals and promises and would experience even the most horrific death to save their ideals. "When you stop being afraid, then you only live" was the phrase Catalina had quoted in one of her letters to Alejo, trying to boost his morale and show him that she was at his side, even from afar. Winter in besieged Madrid had just begun. On the day the barracks fell and a large number of soldiers were slaughtered, it gave the impression that this war would be won by the side of the free citizens. Excited by the victory that he was present, Alejo wrote his news to his beloved who missed him immensely after so many months.

November 1936, Madrid

My life, my soul, my strength,

My beloved Catalina, the struggle for victory continues unabated. It saddens me to see a brother kill a brother. Families have been divided into camps and our division has shown its worst face. The other day, the joy was doubled with the army's push back as I received a letter from Felipe apologizing and wishing me to be alive. I will remain alive for you I promised. I will love you even if the bullet goes through my heart.

Think of me,
your Alejo

For the rest of the war, Madrid was bravely and self-denyingly held by the Republicans. But the Nationalist population was a constant plague on the city that would destroy it from within.

The betrayal

Almost two and a half years of hardship had passed in the capital. Hunger, poverty had resulted in a large number of casualties in Madrid, the news that Barcelona, which had been the strongest stronghold of the Democrats, had fallen into the hands of the Nationalists caused confusion in the left wing, and while they saw that they were losing the battle they continued to defend Madrid to the hilt. But there were also many who gave up their weapons and uniforms and either surrendered or went home. Alejo, however, was not going to take part in either of these two possibilities, and together with his group and a few local inhabitants of Madrid who managed to hold on despite their misery, continued to resist Franco's forces. By land and by air, the bombardments flattened every beauty of the city, which in no way resembled the city Alejo and Felipe had known years before during their studies. But what he thought now was that his best friend was the iron, heavy gun he carried, the cold bullets he loaded to protect him from the enemy.

Among his comrades he had singled out a Greek volunteer, Nicholas, with whom he had developed after two years friendship and fought for the same group. Nicholas was a courageous young man, full of daring and bravery, fighting for a country in which he might not be a citizen but fighting for his beliefs to help Democracy not only in Spain but also in Greece, which a few years later would experience the cruel face of war. His eyes would glow each time and be filled with rage for the enemy. Together with AleJo, they cheered their men and sang of the power of freedom. Among his other virtues was his honesty and he always wanted to express his opinion, he had said in their conversation with Alejo that he fought for people's freedom without caring about their identity whether they were Greek or Spanish.

- Franco fighting his own country can only be called an enemy. He doesn't care about Spain, he just wants to rule, after all how can you be a proper leader if you are fighting your nation?

- It is an honor to fight beside you and die for the victory of the Republic.

It was 31 March 1939 when the weakened Madrid fell into the hands of the executioners. The army entered the city, spreading death among the Republican soldiers and civilians. The slogan "No pasaran" faded from the mouths of the murdered patriots. The battle was lost. Alejo in fear of execution gathered men who were left of his group and with the help of Nicola they fled to Greece to escape arrest and execution. They had to get away as the traitors would hand them over to death. Their human face reacted to the terrorist violence and temporary flight from the country until their traces disappeared was the best solution. The movement of solidarity with the Spanish people by the Greek volunteers would help them towards their escape to Greece. Alejo could not return to Toledo, he was forced to prolong the promise he had made to Catalina; Toledo might at that time have no military value but the Nationalist armies would obviously raids to arrest the Republicans. Greece would have been the best way out since the war from Europe had not yet crossed its borders. Alejo then wrote a letter in which he mentioned to Catalina that he was alive and once the situation was consolidated he would return to her arms, a letter that never reached Catalina's hands.

The days passed agonizingly and Alejo's family had not received any news of him. Doña Sophia had read in the announcements the name of her only son in the list of the missing persons, and she collapsed, so many months and not a single piece of news they thought their son had been lost in the siege of Madrid. His father Don Lorenzo accused himsel of not preventing him from going to fight. Felipe stood by his friend's family, giving courage to his un-just loss. The bad news of Alejo's loss would be relayed by Magda-lena to Catalina as Felipe begged his little sister who knew about the relationship between the two young women to secretly tell Catalina the bad news and stand by her as her friend, her enemy, the one who stole her happiness and didn't care how many people suffered around her. She just wanted to make Catalina erase Alejo from her life once and for all, and so she betrayed her. Her jealousy of her friend's love blinded her and the letter of truth was in her hands. She could never accept that Alejo had fallen in love with another while she loved him since they were little kids. She could not bear to see Catalina happy and herself suffering inwardly for the love that Alejo never returned. The day that the postman brought the letters the treacherous Magdalena begged Don Adrian to give her, her friend's mail as well, on the pretext that she had been ill of late. The peace-loving postman being as tiresome as he was and having seen the girls together several times did the favor, so the truth never reached Catalina. Magdalena read it and decided to hide it deep where Alejo's love would be buried.

On April 1, 1939 the Spanish Civil War had finally come to a definitive end and Franco was the master of the game, plun-ging Spanish cities into his doctrinaire fervor and killing anyone who resisted his regime. Fear and terror intensified throughout the country and many began to emigrate to escape their pre-dicament. The families of Toledo were threatened by oppression, murders and constant control over their lives, but life had to go on so Don Ignacio told his daughter Catalina when he announced his decision to marry her off to a young man of first class and respect in society. Catalina's tears had now dried up, her soul was now broken, she knew that she would make this marriage simply because it was her parents' decision. Her soul, her life was in a thousand pieces, nothing would make sense to her empty heart, no matter how much she resisted this thoughtful marriage nothing would change. Her mother, Doña Marta, who was well aware of what was going on in her beloved daughter's heart, was trying to calm her down and convince her that creating a family would bring joy to her existence. So she put on the silk dress her cousin had given her for her birthday, combed her hair, and went out of her room to meet the young one with his father to ask for her hand, entered the sitting room and could not believe her eyes. The man she was destined to marry was Felipe, Alejo's best friend, how was it possible she wondered to herself.

Felipe had just betrayed his friend's trust and was about to marry the beloved of the unfortunate Alejo. The days passed and everything had been arranged by the two families and Catalina found the courage to talk to Felipe when they were alone at some point, after all he was going to be her husband and she wanted him to trust her.

- *Felipe, I don't know what this marriage is for, but for me it is a way to heal my wounds. But I want to tell you something and then we'll never talk about it again.*
- *No explanation is necessary. I know who you are, and I know exactly what you want to tell me.*

Catalina was puzzled by Felipe's answer and tried to understand what he meant.

- *Alejo was my best friend, but he no longer exists, life goes on and since fate has so arranged that our families agree to this marriage, we will accept and try to be a couple leaving the past behind.*
- *I can't believe that knowing all this you still want this marriage. Felipe, why are you marrying me? Isn't this what you've always secretly wanted inside you since you know who I am?*
- *I know you will never love me, nor will you fall in love with me as you did with Alejo, but if you give me a chance you will see that in a little while there will be laughter and children's voices in this room and maybe then you will love me a little.*
- *I'll agree to try but please don't mention this subject again.*

The wedding day had arrived and everything was ready for the ceremony. Catalina's house was decorated with lovely white lilies which was the bride's favorite flower. But the white veil she was to wear was nothing like the black veil of misery that covered her life. As she prepared she looked in the mirror and a tear of sorrow rolled down her cheek. She remembered that day at Doña Sophia's house when she was rehearsing for her dress and saw Alejo for the first time through the mirror, for seconds she smiled but then her sadness sank again, she sighed and went ahead with her marriage, a marriage that Magdalena would feel no remorse for, a marriage of betrayal.

Dinner with the nightmare

A new life had just begun, a new hope had been born, and everyday life promised to ease the pain of sad Catalina. The memories of the past had to be erased or at least forgotten at all costs. Felipe was trying with all his efforts to create an intimate and comfortable environment with his partner, there may not have been the strong love between them but they had created a relationship based on understanding and honesty between them which was slowly beginning to create a feeling of love. Catalina was now Felipe's wife and she had to accept this and try to make an effort herself to create the family she had always dreamed of. Felipe is a very good man with patience and composure and it didn't take long for Catalina to realize this. She was glad that he had given her the time to recover and apparently that was what brought them together to become a proper couple and begin to share experiences and confidence in what they were building. Catalina felt that she did love Felipe maybe not in the same way that she loved Alejo but with Felipe she felt different, she felt safe with him and supported.

Life between the couple may have flowed harmoniously but there was no lack of tensions in their daily life. Felipe's family and especially Doña Orora were very involved in his life and became pushy and constantly suspicious of Catalina. Besides, she was the only one who had expressed some objections to this marriage despite her kind character. But her overprotectiveness ran into the wall that Felipe had built as he had now created his own family and there had to be a balance and no interference in the life he had with his wife. He was so condescending, so meek that his actions made you feel the confidence of a proper husband, besides, because Felipe had grown up in a strict environment due to Don Pedro's bad temper, he didn't want to follow the same patterns in his own family. All this had to stop at the doorstep of his new home and new life. Magdalena supported Felipe as she had her reasons for not wanting to ruin this marriage under any circumstances. Catalina was not deterred by the intrusive behavior of the Meneses' mother. What she was interested in was making Felipe happy because he was now her family.

The tension in the house was nothing like the tensions that had flared up in Spain. The Civil War had not only flattened a country but had wiped out human relationships. Nothing would ever be the same. Especially the dictatorship imposed by Franco, the product of the victory of his rebellious armies, had resulted in Spain being plunged into a regime of terror where human rights were violated. The country was now isolated and ruined. The war had changed its character and Franco had condemned it to the reality of a vicious circle. The Nationalists were entrenched in power but they were spreading everywhere and were linked to authoritarian attitudes. This is what Don Pedro's guests looked like that afternoon at the Meneses' home. Don Pedro had close associations with them, moreover his character had extreme fluctuations. He was in fact a miniature of them. In the evening of that day there was to be a dinner between the officials and the family. Everything was ready, the clean table-cloths were laid, the smells of the various dishes filled the atmosphere, and wine flowed abundantly into the crystal, carved glasses which adorned the dining-room. This dinner was like an inferno for Catalina, who was forced to sit at the table with the perpetrators responsible for Alejo's loss. At the beginning of the dinner everything was formal and according to the standard of hospitality until Don Pedro started the discussion about the political changes that would be regulated in the country.

-*Senior Diaz, we are pleased that you have honored us with your presence. So what reform we should expect from the regime?*

Facundo Diaz was a general with nationalist sentiments and in the Civil War he had turned against the Reds. He was a vicious man dominated by deceitfulness and evil. He had risen to the upper echelons of power because of his manipulatives and his mask of a good and supposedly noble person trapped many in their extreme ideologies and one of them was Don Pedro, who wanted to get close relations with him so that he could enjoy the favor of power. How sad for an educated man to thus underestimate his own efforts and himself and feel that he is in need of a vile and despicable man simply and only to take advantage of his status. The unscrupulous Facundo Diaz responded with all the arrogance he possessed.

- *Don Pedro, Spain must find its glory! (how ironic that sounded of such an evil man). And to find its glory only a few of us know what it takes. It is not possible to let scum threaten the regime.*

- *Scum meaning the ordinary people you murdered without doing anything? Or the little children you bombed?*

Catalina replied boldly, full of rage at what she was hearing.

- *How dare you insult our guest?*

Don Pedro replied, clearly irritated.

- *Don't worry I understand, Doña Catalina is another victim of misinformation and is confused like the rest of her like-minded people of the same persuasion. You know my lady, it is one thing to have the freedom we stand for and another to use it recklessly as the poor people who were killed in her name believe.*

replied in a devilish tone Facundo Diaz.

- *Senor Diaz, we are all upset and obviously my wife's reaction was somewhat inelegant but believe me she had no intention of offending you.*

Felipe spoke in a voice of reason, gesturing to his wife with his eyes not to continue the conversation and to dine quietly. He was nothing like his wayward father. Felipe had always preferred the diplomatic route, not wanting even himself to show his distaste for Facundo Diaz and the rawness of his thoughts.

-Times change. In Europe, the war has begun and we are obliged not to become the anarchists' pawns.

- What do you mean in Señor Diaz?" asked Magdalena in wonderment.

- 'We have information that many enemies of the regime have fled the country and will surely return at some point. Here in Toledo, we have been informed of a group fighting alongside the other side. In particular, we have under surveillance Lorenzo Carranza. His son was the instigator of some skirmishes and we still haven't tracked him down.

- But we've been informed of his death. Answered Doña Orora.

Catalina on hearing all this news was stunned. She was shocked by the news and her agitation was great.

- Señor Diaz, can you explain to us what exactly do you mean?

asked the treacherous Magdalena in order to clarify the whole announcement, as she felt a fear and anxiety overwhelming her, seeing that her guilty secret was about to be revealed.

- Authoritative sources we have from the surveillance teams stress that Alejo Carranza's team has fled the country the day after our victory in Madrid.

- "What do you ask of us, General Diaz?" asked Felipe calmly.

- 'I know that with this man you have been friends, and I am counting on your cooperation in the capture of the resistance fighters?

- You mean to tell us that there is a chance that Alejo is alive?

Magdalena asked, playing the theatre of her ignorance.

- Unfortunately I cannot know this so I ask for your help in case he contacts you.

- Then so be it!

was Felipe's dry response to this extreme suggestion by Facundo Diaz. But Felipe knew deep in his heart that he was not going to do so, and his answer was ambiguous. All he could think was that if Alejo lived his life would be shattered in seconds, but he would not surrender his friend to death. Catalina, obviously annoyed and disgusted by the dinner of shame, rose frantically from the table and left with the fury of a passionate woman. It was a great dis-respect and insult to her reaction that they tried to excuse it as a petulant behavior. Magdalena lowered her eyes and sank into her thoughts while Felipe looked the general in the eye and the dinner continued.

The return of the past

After that dinner of shame, doubts had overwhelmed Catalina about Alejo's survival. The situation between the Meneses family was tense because of their daughter-in-law's spontaneous reaction to openly insulting General Diaz. Felipe was trying to smooth the tension by supporting his wife as he was opposed to his father's views and his steep behavior that he just wanted to enjoy the favor of power. This vanity, however, was not embraced by Magdalena either, although she was worried that her intrigue might one day be revealed and in no way would she want to endanger Alejo's life. Any Republicans who had survived the Civil War would surrender and be executed as an example. In order to avoid being targeted, Felipe suggested to Catalina that they should not pursue the events so that there would be no bad developments and they could go on with their lives as normal. Catalina agreed, but deep down her instincts warned her that things would turn out differently.

World War II had broken out and Europe was the chessboard of two rival ideologies. Although the Civil War was a bloody bastion of war, Franco's Spain, due to the depletion of his army on the battlefields, did not formally join the war. Alejo, who was in Greece, seeing the situation in the country take a different turn, decided to return secretly to Toledo as the trains would soon be carrying soldiers to the war front. So Alejo greeted Nicola, thanked him for his hospitality and for his support during the war. He knew now that he had a friend outside the country's borders, a true friend with bravery and determination.

- *I hope the war in Europe will end and we will see each other again, friend. Our Democracy will win this time, you'll see.*
- *It's been an honor, Nicola, to fight beside you, you're already a hero. There are hard days ahead, I hope to meet my people soon.*

So Alejo set off on his way back, not knowing what awaited him. The letter he had sent to Catalina was his only hope that his beloved would be waiting for him.

In the Carranza household life went on under the grief of their lost only son, unbeknownst to either Don Lorenzo or Doña Sophia that the provincial security guards were searching for traces of his survival. It was a winter morning and atmosphere had spread its mist over the city. It was very difficult to make out anyone's figure in the streets of Toledo. It was the best cover there could have been that day. Alejo, after several days of travel and exhausting journeys by whatever means he could find, managed to find himself at the entrance to the province. The beard of so many months made him look unrecognizable and so hardly anyone could recognize him. He walked through the alleys of the town, and whenever a curious person looked at him he either hid his eyes or proceeded to hide in some narrow passage. His footsteps would lead him out of his father's house to where, from a distance, he would see his father, who had gone out to protect some vegetables in the garden from the chill air that had begun to rise over the country. Then he heard the front doorbell ring, someone had opened the wooden garden door, he looked up and then he saw him.

- *It was not possible. How could it be possible? I can't believe you're alive, son.*

Alejo then ran into Don Lorenzo's arms and they cried with emotion and relief, they were together again.

- Sophia, Sophia, run quickly.

Doña Sophia had a small lamp lit beside her sewing machine and was gazing at some clothes that had been brought to her for mending. It was the only way to keep her mind off things. It kept her hands and her mind busy so she could forget. At the sound of Lorenzo's voices she immediately ran outside fearing something bad was happening to him, she couldn't believe her eyes, she was experiencing a miracle, her little angel was alive and had returned.

- My child, my soul, my boy where have you been for so long? What happiness this is for a mother to see her child alive. We feared you had been swallowed up by the Civil War monster.

- Now i'm here mother, and that's what matters. But let's go inside now because someone might be watching us.

After Alejo had rested, washed and groomed his face by shaving his beard, he returned to his old self and recounted the adventure of their life all these months and the atrocities of the Civil War in Madrid for the past two years.

-While I was in Greece, my thoughts were here with you in Toledo. Life has got worse, Europe is at war. If I went back immediately I would be arrested.

- Boy, you're not entirely safe here either. The other day in Meneses there was a general asking about you.

- Well, tomorrow I'll visit Felipe and surprise him. He'll go crazy when he sees me.

- But be careful, my soul, there have been rumors about his father's connections.

- Mother, we know very well that Felipe has nothing to do with it.

-You can go, my child, and you will hear the good news of your child-hood friend's marriage.

- I can't wait to see who is the one who can bear my friend.

- In fact, your father has learned that Felipe has interceded so that you will not be attacked in case you return.

- And here I am. After all, Felipe is a friend and deserves a wise and good wife.

The next day, Alejo, not knowing that the unpleasant surprise would be in store for him, set out for Felipe's office. He knew how he would find him in his hundreds of glass jars, inventing various medicines and remedies. Catalina had lately been spending a lot of time with her husband. Especially in the doctor's office she was helping him, but she also enjoyed him explaining various medical procedures to her. Even that morning she was particularly warm with him and distracted him from his work with various kisses and caresses, they looked like a deeply in love couple who had found the secret of happiness, until the door knocked.

- *Please come in.*

Felipe exclaimed, pulling Catalina from his arms to greet the man who was knocking on the door of the doctor's office. Some patient it could have been he thought. When Alejo appeared at the door, they were both speechless. Were they seeing a ghost or was it reality?

- *Are you alive?*

Felipe asked, who had completely lost it.

- *Of course I am. I came to surprise you, but I guess you surprised me. I imagine the lady next to you is your wife.*

- *Alejo, let me explain,* said Felipe.

- *'Explain what, your betrayal or that your plan has succeeded? It's all yours, the lady doesn't even deserve my contempt.*

Catalina with tears in her eyes and overwhelmed was trying to encourage me to say a word.

- *How is it possible?"* she spoke in a trembling voice.

- *How is it possible what; that you betrayed me; that you are a liar?*

- *We didn't know. We all thought you were lost in Madrid. This marriage...*

- *I don't want to hear a word from you. Your mockery knows no bounds, and you, Felipe, who do you think you are? A coward, or do you think that with your acquaintances you will destroy my freedom? Better that their power should kill me, less will be this pain than the pain of your treachery. I wish you happiness, you are both made of the same stuff, treacherous and liars.*

Catalina lowered her eyes and burst into sobs. Alejo strode towards the exit, slamming the door and his anger and rage had gotten the better of him. He couldn't believe the twist of fate, the woman he adored had married his best friend. The price of betrayal would be high. Alejo may not have had a thirst for revenge inside of him, but frustration overwhelmed every aspect of his life. All his dreams had been shattered like glass that, when it falls, breaks into a thousand pieces. As he made his way to the front door of the garden that was farthest away he heard a woman's voice behind him calling to him.

- *How glad I am to see you alive. I always knew you'd come back, I could feel it.*

She said Magdalena hugging him tightly.

- *I'd rather not come back, Magdalena.*

 - *What's wrong with you? I think I know what's wrong with you. You heard about the wedding, didn't you?*

- *Yes, I've come to say my wishes.*

- *Alejo, don't blame Felipe. That girl wasn't made for you, see how she treated you and don't blame my brother right away. In time you'll see that she did things for you.*

- *Just buy his conscience.*

- *Let's go for a walk. I want you to tell me everything.*

The headlines of the end

Not long after, and despite Don Pedro Meneses' objections, Carranzas and the Meneses would become a family as Alejo and Magdalena discovered their love for each other and decided to make it official with their marriage. A marriage that would be based on a secret, a lie. Catalina tried to be smiling and cheerful in the world but inside she was mourning her lost love. She in no way wanted to embarrass Felipe, who had been so kind and supportive to her. The newlyweds had arranged how they would move to Paris, to the house of aunt Maria Carmen, who had now given it to Alejo as a wedding present, since she had no descendants. In the first days of married life, Magdalena lived her dream. Alejo was now hers and her father had accepted him despite his past in the Civil War and decided to protect him since he saw his daughter's love for him. Catalina felt herself dying inside every time she saw them together and for her all that was left was Alejo's disgust for her for constantly avoiding her.

Felipe seeing these reactions was convinced that the old

love would not flare up and that they had all created new paths in their lives. But the mind may forget, but the heart never. One night, however, and while they were all asleep, Catalina took the opportunity to approach Alejo and speak to him. She knew that he always sat late by the fireplace and read by the light of the flame. In the quiet of the night there was the sound of footsteps, Alejo jumped up in fright to locate the source of the noise and then he saw Catalina. He felt somewhat strange, beautifully strange that it was her and not Magdalena.

- *Sorry if I startled you I wasn't asleep and came down to get some air.*
The silence fell as if it was the only tolerable thing between them, which created an atmosphere of awkwardness.

- *I wonder if you'll ever forgive me Alejo?*
Catalina said in a heartbreaking voice and with eyes full of anticipation for a positive answer.

- *Every time I hear footsteps approaching I wish it was you.*
This forgiveness was a deliverance to Catalina's aching soul. They might not be together anymore but she knew their love could not stop, it was more than a feeling, it was the ultimate. But how to extinguish a passion that survives even in a war? Then Alejo gently took Catalina's hand and placed it on his chest and said to her:

- *You can feel it, it's my heart and it's broken but you can feel that the pieces are now put together and that's because you are you. I cannot with any strength resist you.*
With a sudden movement he pulled her towards him and kissed her with such passion, such intensity that the memories ignited a flame that would be capable of burning anything in its path. From that night onward there was an awkwardness that would have betrayed what had

what had happened. Love might break down walls, cross seas, tear down fortresses, but Alejo would never compromise the morals of the woman he loved to live with her for something forbidden. Now he belonged to Magdalena and she to Felipe.

Love lives may have been mixed up at home, but the biggest problem was the impending war. World War II was to be the biggest and most destructive conflict. Spain's and Franco's questionable attitude about the country's future in the war reinforced Alejo's decision to move with Magdalena to Paris. In this way he would both avoid possible arrest by regime gunmen and end any attraction with Catalina. But events would take a different turn and Magdalena's intrigue would sooner or later be exposed with disastrous results. A few days before his departure for France, and while Alejo was preparing the last details of the journey, he found among some of his wives' books a letter of his own written the day after the fall of Madrid to Catalina. In this letter he explained that he was alive and that he would return from Greece. So he wondered how it was possible that such a confidential letter could be hidden in Magdalena's room and then he understood everything. His eyes darkened, anger overcame him and he almost lost his temper, he was sure that the woman he had married was not who she seemed. His thoughts were confused and his life was full of lies and hypocrisy. He immediately ran to find Magdalena to give him some explanations.

- *What does that mean, Magdalena? What is your plan? Did you want to live in the misery of so many people? Why did you do it? Why?*
- *I will not apologize for something that belongs to the past and you'd do well to throw that letter away, it changes nothing, it proves nothing, the choices have been made.*
- *You are wrong the choices are now being made. Our journey together ends here. My God, how sneaky you were.*

Magdalena looked at him, full of envy and hatred, and her grief had built up so that her cycle of anger was leading her down the most difficult path of revenge. A path that has no turning back and irreparably pollutes the souls of men. Without wasting time and with her mind clouded, she wanted to punish Alecjo in every possible way to repay him for abandoning her with the price of betrayal. So she betrayed Alejo to the Nationalists with the help of General Diaz, thus signing his condemnation. He collaborated with the enemy to set a trap for his arrest for his participation in the Civil War with the forces of the Resistance, without ever making its involvement known. But the irony of life had yet to play its last card.

Alejo thought how this letter was the proof that would bring redemption to his life beside Catalina. Without wasting time he went to meet her and announce his separation with Magdalena and also to propose a new beginning away from everyone.

- I can't believe it. How could Magdalena do such a thing? She was my friend. How could she? It's too late to think about why.

- Nothing is too late, Catalina. Come with me. Let's get out of here.

- Are you crazy? Have you thought about how many people we're going to hurt?

- Did they think when they hurt us? We go back, stay in here a little longer and we'll fall apart.

- What about Felipe?

- He is also a victim of his sister, but when given the choice he betrayed our friendship. He didn't just break it, he tore it apart from the foundation. My desire for you will not be reduced to ashes no matter how much I am burned by marriages that should never have happened. Tonight I'll be waiting for you outside the main church. I have waited for you for a long time Catalina and tonight I will wait for you for the last time in the hope that you will show up.

The night spread its veils over the magical city of Toledo. This picturesque province of the Iberian Peninsula with its romantic character would witness pain, true love and conspiracy. Alejo greeted their parents, kissed them, hugged them and left for the church of Santo Tome. The Meneses' house was in turmoil after his sudden departure. Magdalena had not regretted her decision to denounce him to authorities. No one had noticed Catalina's absence except Felipe who saw her sneak out the back door. He had already figured it all out and didn't have the strength to react. Had Catalina chosen Alejo, or had she not? In the darkness and among the rustling leaves, he saw Catalina arrive, she was so beautiful and restless at the same time that no one would see her.

- I knew you would come. I felt it.

Alejo told her, hugging her and noticing her wet eyes, full of tears.

- I'm pregnant. I'm expecting Felipe's child.

- What? And you came all the way here for what, Catalina? To see me in pain, humiliated? What exactly?

- I can't leave Felipe. It's not just the child, with him I feel safe. This has been my life for a long time.
- Do you love him?

Alejo asked, feeling a stab through his heart and the curtain of his life falling. But before Catalina could give her answer, a group of police guards raiding the place arrested Alejo on the charge of being an enemy of the regime and would take him to jail. It was also the last time she saw him. She let out a loud scream, a howl of pain and then she felt two hands embrace her, she turned around and saw Felipe. He had watched her when he heard of Magdalena's betrayal as he knew something like this would happen.

- You don't have to explain anything to me. I know and heard it all. We'll live together, alone, just the two of us, alone with our child. The three of us as a family, only you will exist for me.

Catalina understood then that it was her choices, although she loved Alejo, with Felipe she had imagined her future. Alejo was never executed. He managed to escape and rumor has it that he fled to Greece where he experienced the pain of betrayal and the end of a glorious love affair. Everyone had made their choices. Alejo as a revolutionary character couldn't help but fight until the end of his life for freedom anyway it never betrayed him, at least he knew Catalina would be happy.

- Amazing mom. How much love, how much pain there is.
- The Civil War, my daughter, is the worst kind of suffering. It changes people and lives. It ruthlessly extorts human happiness and gives way to misery.

I was really impressed by the story of grandma's life Catalina. Now it explained all the melancholy attitudes that grandma sometimes had.

- After all, mother, you were right. We each live our choices the way we wish, but in love and friendship and freedom it is worth trying.

Spain for nearly three decades went through the darkness of brutal dictatorship. It was 1975 when the country breathed the air of Democracy again.

The End

Acknowledgement

First of all, I would like to thank God for giving me the opportunity and guidance to achieving my goal. Then I would like to thank my family for their upbringing of me and their tireless efforts and support in every path I take to achieve my dreams and goals. I am so blessed and honored to have them both as my parents. I want to show my thankfulness for their love and support over the years. Thank you for guiding me in learning and doing everything possible to walk in the path of greatness.

Made in the USA
Middletown, DE
29 March 2022

63352922R00033